Jungles sound very exciting, with their lions and tigers, elephants and monkeys. Rain forests are full of strange trees and tropical flowers. For most of us, though, they are very far away. But all round us, in every country, there is a world of nature just as interesting as jungles and forests, on a smaller scale.

Exploring this world you can see nature at work. Here are some ideas to help you to enter the world of nature, not just by looking but by doing.

KEEPING WOODLICE

Woodlice are small animals living under stones, damp logs, rotting bark or in other moist places like compost heaps or damp moss clumps. If you disturb them, some will roll up into a ball, and some will scuttle off to a dark corner.

There are many different kinds of woodlice. One of the most common is small, oval-shaped and grey. Woodlice are not insects. They have jointed bodies and many jointed legs covered with tough skin. They are grouped with other jointed shell-bearing animals like crabs and lobsters.

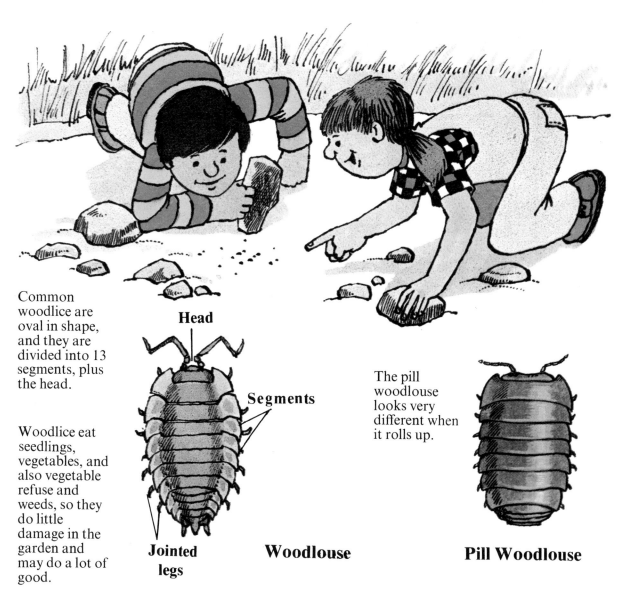

Common woodlice are oval in shape, and they are divided into 13 segments, plus the head.

Woodlice eat seedlings, vegetables, and also vegetable refuse and weeds, so they do little damage in the garden and may do a lot of good.

Head

Segments

Jointed legs

Woodlouse

The pill woodlouse looks very different when it rolls up.

Pill Woodlouse

What You Do

1. Put a layer of damp soil, about 6 cms. deep, on the bottom of a flat, clear plastic box.

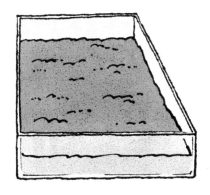

2. Add some dead leaves and pieces of wood bark, and, if you have room, a medium size stone.

3. Look for some woodlice under a large stone or a damp log, or under rotting bark.

4. Collect about 20, counting them if you can, and put them at once into your box. Cover them with a lid.

5. Keep the soil damp, not wet. Give them fresh food every day – a fresh cabbage or lettuce leaf, or a slice of raw carrot or potato.

6. Woodlice like the dark. If you want to watch them, stick a piece of red paper over a torch, and watch them in a dark room.

7. After a couple of weeks, empty your box, and try to count the woodlice again before putting them back into the garden.

3

SETTING UP A WORMERY

There are many different types of worms, some red or pink, some brown or grey, and some almost blue or green. All worms are very useful in the soil.

Many worms eat soil. They digest the tiny pieces of decaying plant material in it, and the waste soil passes through their bodies, changing in texture as it does so. You can see these small lumps of broken up soil on the surface. They are called **worm-casts**. These worm-casts provide manure for the plants. See how many worm-casts you can count in a patch of lawn.

The burrows and the worm-casts break up the hard soil and make it easier for plant roots to grow down into the soil and provide the plant with food and anchorage.

Earthworm

Worms also pull down leaves and plant stalks into the ground and eat or bury them. What they leave decomposes and adds goodness to the soil.

Without worms, plants would not grow so well, and other animals would find it difficult to survive in the soil.

Worm-cast

Worm burrow

What To Do

1. Get a fairly large, transparent, plastic box, with a lid, or a large jam jar.

Make small holes in the lid, or in the jam jar cover.

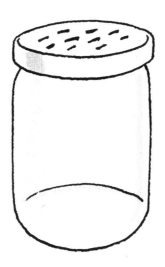

2. Put a layer of darkish garden soil at the bottom.

Then add a layer of sand, about 4 cms. deep. Then make another layer of dark soil.

You can have as many layers as you want, but there must be empty space at the top for air.

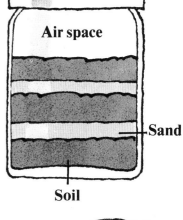

Air space

Sand

Soil

3. Dig in the garden for about six to eight worms. Find the big, fat, pink ones if you can.

If you go out with a torch on a warm, damp night, you will find them all over the lawn.

4. Put the worms in the box or jar. Then put on the lid or jam jar cover so that the worms can't get out.

5. Stick a strip of paper on the side of the jam jar or box with the positions of the soil and the sand marked on it.

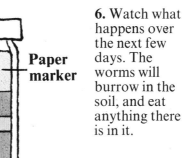

Paper marker

6. Watch what happens over the next few days. The worms will burrow in the soil, and eat anything there is in it.

Gradually, they will mix up the sand in with the soil. You may also see worm casts on the surface.

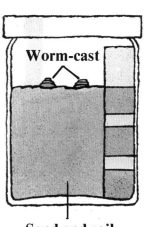

Worm-cast

Sand and soil mixed together

7. When you have seen how the worms do their work, return them to the garden.

BREEDING BUTTERFLIES

Butterflies are beautiful and interesting insects. Butterflies play a part in the food chain because they are eaten, particularly in their caterpillar stage, by other insects, birds, reptiles and other animals.

A butterfly is an insect that has **complete metamorphosis.** This means that it has **four** distinct stages in its life-cycle:– **1. The egg 2. The caterpillar 3. The chrysalis 4. The adult butterfly.**

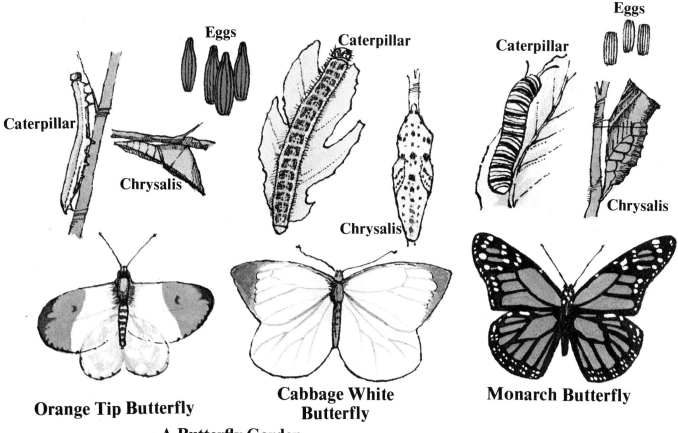

Orange Tip Butterfly

Cabbage White Butterfly

Monarch Butterfly

A Butterfly Garden

The best way to encourage butterflies is to plant a butterfly garden. In it there have to be two kinds of plants. One is to attract the butterflies in summer when they need nectar. The other is the one on which they lay their eggs, so that the caterpillars can feed on the leaves. For example, the Peacock Butterfly lays eggs on nettles and likes to visit Michaelmas Daisies and other garden flowers for nectar.

6

How To Breed Butterflies Yourself

To breed butterflies yourself you need some simple apparatus.

A plant pot full of soil
A small jar full of water
Some cotton wool
A cylinder of clear plastic or perspex
A piece of gauze

Gauze

What You Do

1. First of all, get your apparatus ready.

Jam jar full of water

Plant pot full of soil

2. Put the cylinder of plastic round the plant pot and jar.

Cover the top with the gauze held in place by a rubber band.

Plastic cylinder

3. In late spring or early summer, look for the eggs on the undersides of leaves.

Both Peacock and Tortoiseshell Butterfly eggs are laid on the underside of nettle leaves.

4. Cut off the whole stem with leaves and eggs on it, and put the stem in the small jar of water. Plug the top of the jar with cotton wool, so the caterpillars, when they emerge, will not fall into the water.

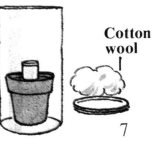

Cotton wool

7

5. When the eggs have hatched, you must give the caterpillars fresh food every day. Use the same plant you found the eggs on to feed them.

Put the new leaves next to the old ones. The caterpillars will find their way to the fresh food.

6. Keep 3 or 4 caterpillars and take the rest back to the plant where you found the eggs.

7. Keep the container clean and away from sunlight.

8. After a few weeks, each caterpillar will move to the wall of the container, or the food plant, and hang itself up by a tail-pad of silk before changing to a chrysalis. Some species will burrow in the soil.

9. Peacock or Tortoiseshell butterflies ought to emerge in June or July.
If your eggs belong to other species, try and identify them in a butterfly book, and find out when they emerge.

10. When your butterflies have emerged, release them into the garden.

8

HOW TO MAKE PLASTER CASTS OF ANIMAL TRACKS

Many wild animals are very shy, and many only come out at night. Although you may not see the animals themselves, you can look out for signs that show where they have visited, and what trails they have followed. You can look out for their **tracks**, or footprints.

In wet weather, or by streams and ditches, look for their tracks in soft mud. In winter, look for them in hard snow.

Rat

Cat

Dog

Fox

Badger

Hedgehog

Weasel

Deer

Rabbit

Pheasant

Sparrow

Some animals, such as deer, badgers and rabbits, usually follow paths, whereas cats and foxes avoid existing trails and make their own routes. Some animals, like rats and weasels, try to keep to cover. Look for their tracks by hedges and ditches.

Look out also for bird tracks in the mud or snow.

9

What You Need

1. A bag of Plaster of Paris (from a chemist or art shop).

2. A basin.

3. A jug of water.

4 A stick or spoon.

5. Some strips of cardboard or cardboard boxes.

6. A sheet of newspaper.

What You Do

1. First of all, decide which prints you want to make a plaster cast of.

2. Make a frame of the cardboard, putting it round the print you want to take.

3. Quickly mix your plaster by putting some of it in the basin, gradually adding the water, and mixing it with your stick or spoon.

It should be like thick cream with no lumps.

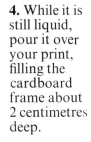

4. While it is still liquid, pour it over your print, filling the cardboard frame about 2 centimetres deep.

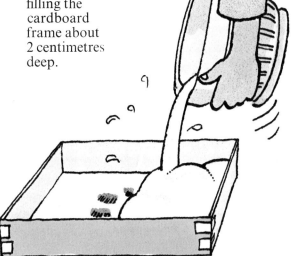

10

5. Cover it over to avoid disturbance, and leave it to harden. It should take about 15 minutes, but leave it even longer if you can.

6. Take it up, with the soil still sticking to it, and wrap it in the newspaper to protect it.

7. When you get home, gently ease off the mud with a little running water, and a soft brush if necessary.

8. Write on the back where and when you found it, and, if you can, which animal it belongs to.

Making good casts does take practice, but is great fun.

Another way you can make a cast is to pour your liquid into a cardboard box, wait until it is beginning to set, and then place a leaf or twig on it.

You can take a print of your pet's paw in this way as long as you wash its paw immediately afterwards.

Badger 3/9/78

If you make a cast like this, when it is hard, you can use the print as a mould and make as many copies as you want.

11

COLLECTING FEATHERS

All birds have a lot of feathers. A big bird, like a swan, may have more than twenty-five thousand feathers. Even a budgerigar or a canary may have up to two thousand.

Feathers probably evolved from the scales of birds' ancestors – the reptiles. The flight feathers on the wings and on the tail are strong, stiff structures, and yet are 'as light as a feather'.

Look at a wing feather under a magnifying glass and you will see that it is incredibly complex. Feathers are light, strong and flexible. These are all very important qualities if the bird is to control its flight.

Where To Look

You can find feathers anywhere. Birds drop them in gardens, or in city streets and squares. When you go for a walk in the country, look for them in fields and woods. On the seashore there will be different kinds, from seabirds. The best time to find feathers is when the birds are moulting, after they have finished the yearly task of nest-building and rearing their young.

If you visit zoos and bird sanctuaries the keepers will often save feathers from exotic birds for you.

The inner feathers are soft and downy, to keep the bird warm.

The outer and stronger feathers are used for flight, and to keep the bird dry.

With a magnifying glass you can see how complex a feather is.

Coloured feathers help to disguise the bird from its enemies.

Coloured feathers are sometimes used for display, when the male bird is trying to attract the female.

Peacocks, Turkeys, Birds of Paradise, and many more, have the most lovely tail feathers.

Make a collection of different feathers. You can stick them into a notebook with sticky tape, with a note as to when and where you found them, and if you can, which bird they belong to.

The male is nearly always more colourful than the female.

Magpie

You could also stick a selection of different feathers onto a piece of black paper to put on your wall.

Curlew

Jay

Woodpecker

Partridge

Kingfisher

Pheasant

Mallard

13

COLLECTING SPIDERS' WEBS

There are thousands of different kinds of spiders in the world. You can find many of them in almost any area of a garden or park. Some spiders, like the house spider, you will also find living in your home.

House Spider

You can find spiders' webs round the house or in a shed, and also on bushes, between plants, on fences and between gateposts outside. Most of the large, spiral webs you will find are built by the garden spider.

Garden Spider

You may be able to watch the spider weaving her web. It may take her up to two hours to complete. The spider constructs these webs using two different kinds of silk, which it produces from spinnerets at the end of its abdomen. One kind of silk is dry, the other sticky. Look at the web to see how beautifully it is made.

How To Collect A Spiders' Web

1. You will need some fine white paint spray, a sheet of black card, and some clear 'film wrap' – the one used for cooking will do.

2. Make sure the spider is not in the middle of the web.

3. Spray the web gently with the white paint spray.

4. Then, from **behind**, hold the sheet of black card and gently bring it forwards until it holds the web.

5. Leave it for a while to let the paint dry, then cover it with the clear film.

You will find that with practice, you will be able to collect the web without breaking it.

6. It is very difficult to collect a whole web. Photographing webs is also worth trying.

Another way you can collect webs is to collect a fragment of a web, and then try and draw in the rest of it.

7. If you spoil a web despite all your care you may be able to watch the spider repairing it.

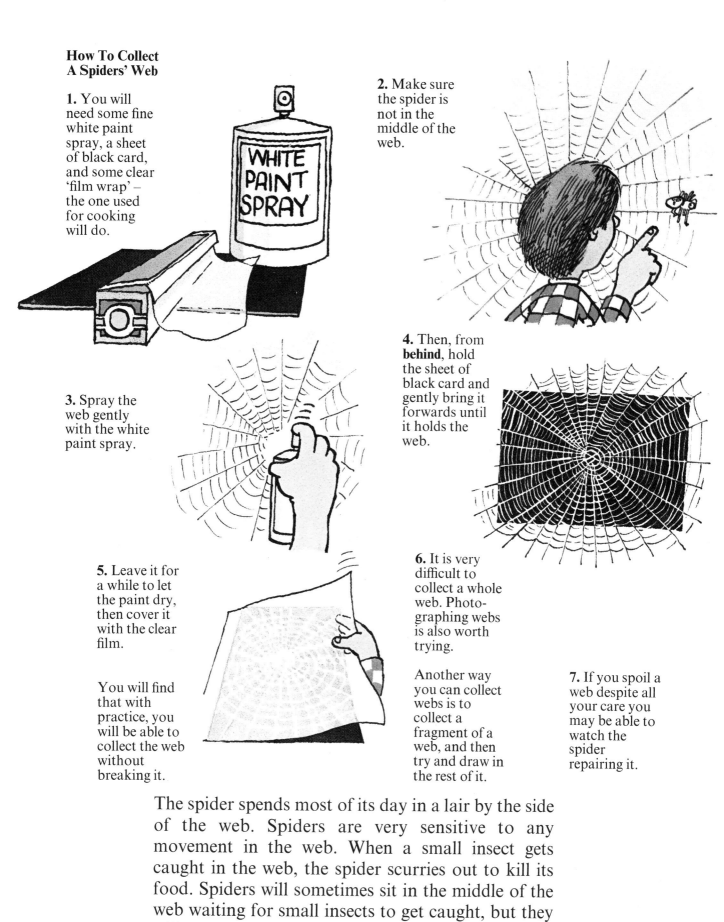

The spider spends most of its day in a lair by the side of the web. Spiders are very sensitive to any movement in the web. When a small insect gets caught in the web, the spider scurries out to kill its food. Spiders will sometimes sit in the middle of the web waiting for small insects to get caught, but they will not do so for long as it is dangerous for them in the day when birds are about.

15

WHAT CAN YOU FIND BY A POND?

What To Look Out for:—

A small natural pond can be a most interesting habitat for wildlife of all kinds.

Some ponds are very neglected and dirty, full of tin cans, rusting bicycles and rotting weeds. Some are much too big and deep for you to work on. Try and find a small shallow pond.

1. The **mallard duck** is the most common bird on such ponds.

2. Moorhens are easily frightened, and will start away if disturbed, even leaving their little black chicks behind.

3. Swans and **coots** need a lot of swimming space.

4. Herons like undisturbed places.

5. Swallows and **martins** collect mud from ponds to build their nests.

6. Dragonflies dart about shining, up to 10 centimetres across.

7. In the evenings, there are often swarms of **midges** above the water.

8. Hidden below there is a whole world of small plants and animals – beetles, spiders, snails, and the larvae of many insects.

Silver Birch

Alder

Swallow

Dragonfly

Heron

Coot

Swan

Water Lilies

Mallard

Midges

Marsh Marigolds

Moorhen

Rushes

There is usually a rich variety of plant life on and around the pond.

Take with you – your rubber boots, a piece of rope, and a notebook and pencil.

What You Do

1. Put one end of the rope just in the water, at the very edge, and then lay it out away from the water up the bank.

2. Count the number of different plants you can find on either side of the rope.

3. Draw a plan of the plants. Write in the names of the ones you know.

Make little drawings of any plants you do not recognise, with any little details you notice such as colour or shape. Later you can look these plants up and identify them.

Look Out For:—

1. Yellow or white **water-lilies**.

2. Water-weeds, floating on the top, rooted, or submerged.

3. Rushes, or the **greater reedmace** may be round the shore.

4. The **yellow flag** or **iris** may flower among the rushes.

5. Are there any **marsh marigolds (kingcups)** or **forget-me-nots**?

6. Can you recognize the creamy scented **meadowsweet** or the pink spikes of **purple loosestrife**?

7. Willow trees like to grow near water.

8. Silver birches and **alders** thrive in marshland.

9. Briars, brambles and **hawthorns** grow on drier land.

If you do this with different ponds, you will see how much flowers and plants vary in different parts of the country.

Willow

Briars, brambles and hawthorns

Greater Reedmace

Mallard

Moorhen

Dragonfly

Yellow Flag

Purple Loosestrife

Water-weeds

17

TESTING A STREAM

Streams are very different from ponds. Running water creates different conditions for the wildlife in and around the water.

You can measure the speed the water flows at.

What You Do

1. Mark out a convenient length of the stream – say 50 metres – and then with a stop-watch time how long it takes a ping-pong ball to travel that distance in the water.

Then you can work out the rate of flow.

A stream or river is also different from a pond or lake in that it flows through many different sorts of areas, perhaps from high mountains through towns, down to the sea. During this journey, it can get very dirty. Soil is carried along, and the stream may get silted up. If it runs near towns and factories, it may be used for getting rid of industrial waste products, sometimes very harmful to wildlife, as well as sewage.

All over the world, big efforts are being made to clean up rivers. You can see for yourself what the problem is if you test a fairly shallow stream near your home – one not too deep or swift, and one you can visit from time to time. You can find out whether it is fit for fish and other animals to live in, or whether they have all died out.

You Will Need

1. A fishing net of very fine mesh, (perhaps made from a piece of nylon cloth) at the end of a good, long stick.
2. A shallow dish, best with a white bottom, so that specimens show up well.
3. A notebook to record your findings.
4. A magnifying glass or a hand lens.

What You Do

1. At the edge of the stream take several sweeps through the water with your net, and empty anything you catch into the dish.

2. Let the mud settle, and then see whether you have caught any small fish or other animals.

Do this several times.

Stonefly Nymph

Look For:—

a) The Stonefly Nymph. This is the young stage of the adult Stonefly, and it can only live in **clean water**.

If the water is clean you may find lots of other small creatures. Draw them in your notebook, and see if you can find out what they are when you get home.

b) The Freshwater Shrimp. You may not find the nymph, and get the Freshwater Shrimp instead.

This shows that there is probably a small amount of pollution in the water, but not enough to kill all life.

3. If after several trials you find no animals at all, and are quite sure of this, then you have another detective problem, of **how** the water got so dirty.

Freshwater Shrimp

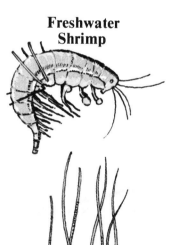

Sludge Worms

You may be able to explore whether there is an outfall of sewage near your trial ground, or another dirty stream entering further up.

c) Sludge Worms and **Rat-tailed Maggots**. These can live in **very dirty** water.

If these are present in your catch, and nothing else, it shows the water is very dirty indeed.

Rat-tailed Maggots

4. If you can find out the source of the trouble you may be able to persuade someone to do something about it!

19

HOW TO TAKE BARK RUBBINGS

Trees grow in many different shapes and sizes. Their branches and leaves are also different. Just as different are the patterns made by the ridges and hollows of their **bark**. The thick bark of a tree protects its structure, just as the skin or hide of an animal protects it. If the bark is seriously damaged, the tree will die.

All plants need sunlight to survive. Trees get their share of the sunlight by growing tall. The trunk of the tree has to be very strong to support it. The bark not only protects the tree, but also gives it strength.

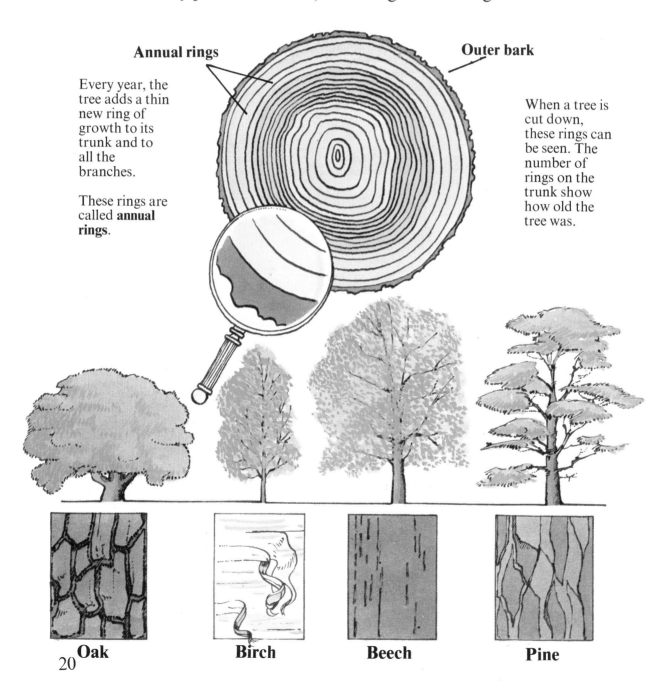

Annual rings

Outer bark

Every year, the tree adds a thin new ring of growth to its trunk and to all the branches.

These rings are called **annual rings**.

When a tree is cut down, these rings can be seen. The number of rings on the trunk show how old the tree was.

Oak

Birch

Beech

Pine

20

You can make bark rubbings to show the different patterns found on different trees.

What You Do

1. Hold a piece of strong white paper against the trunk of a tree and mark the top with a T and the bottom with a B so you know which way up it should be.

2. Gently rub over the paper with a piece of black wax crayon. Don't press the paper or crayon into the cracks. You are trying to get an impression of the ridges, and these should stand up black against the white gaps of the hollows.

OAK 29/6/77

3. Put the name of the tree on the paper and the date you made the rubbing, so that you can make a collection.

4. How many different patterns can you find?

MAKE A SLEEP PILLOW

Many herbs and flowers are used for cooking, for medicine and for making perfume. They can also be used to make a sleep pillow.

A sleep pillow is a small, flat pillow stuffed with sweet-scented dried herbs and placed under your usual pillow to send you to sleep with its lovely smell.

What You Do

1. First you collect your herbs and flowers.

2. Pick as many rose petals as you can. Scented, old-fashioned roses are best.

3. Collect lavender heads as soon as the flowers have finished and the seeds are there.

Lavender

4. Add any other leaves with a sweet smell–mint, rosemary and sweet briar are a few to look out for.

Herbs such as thyme and camomile are useful, and may be growing in your garden.

5. The leaves of the hop plant are almost best of all, as they have a sleepy smell, but you will probably have to grow your own plants if you want them.

6. Dry everything as it is collected. If you keep a tray in a warm part of the airing cupboard you can add petals and leaves each day as you get them.

Don't have too thick a layer. Take some out as it becomes really dry. A few days in the airing cupboard should be enough.

7. While the leaves and petals are drying, (and make sure they really are powdery and dry), make a little bag of cotton, any size you like – 15 cm. × 20 cm. is large enough, but you can make it bigger if you wish.

9. Make another bag, a little larger than your pillow, in a pretty material.

Leave one end open, and put your sleep pillow in its cover to keep it clean.

Sleep pillows are nice for yourself, and they make very nice Christmas and birthday presents.

8. Stuff the bag as tight as you can, and then sew up the open edge.

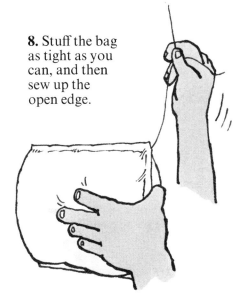

23

BUILD A FLOWERING WALL

If you have a stone or a brick wall where you live, you can turn it into a flowering garden. You can make your wall into a flower bed because so many plants have adapted themselves to living with very little rain or soil.

Go and look at old walls near you, especially round churches or ruins, and bridges, if you can. You will be amazed at how many different kinds of plants you can find growing in and on the wall. In one wall, in England, over 200 kinds were found. You will also find many kinds of insects and other small creatures living on the wall, including snails, slugs, spiders and woodlice. Mice may live in crevices near the bottom, and there may also be a bird's nest among the plants growing on it.

What You Do

1. Grow climbing plants along the bottom – ivy, honeysuckle, wild clematis or bramble. Climbing plants grow upwards to get their share of the sunlight.

Climbing plants

Flowering Wall

2. On top of the wall grow plants that hang downwards, either in pots, (make sure they don't fall off), or in pockets of soil.

Hanging plants

Nasturtiums, aubretia and alyssum all have bright flowers and will grow in cascades down your wall.

3. On the wall itself, there are a large number of plants you can plant in the crevices, such as houseleeks, stonecrop, moss, saxifrages, or any small rock plants. Wallflowers and ferns grow very well on walls. Snapdragons and harebells also grow well.

Saxifrage

Harebell

Stonecrop

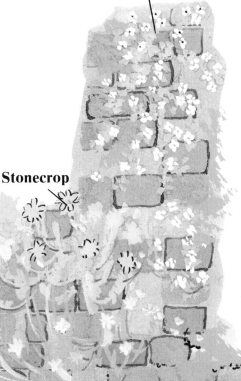

4. If you hang an old boot, or kettle, (with a couple of holes in the bottom so the rain runs out), hidden among your plants, a robin is almost sure to nest there.

Old boot

Old broom

5. An old-fashioned broom made of twigs or a bundle of pea-sticks may attract some other small bird to nest.

GROW YOUR OWN PORRIDGE

Every year farmers have to prepare the land, put seed in, look after the growing crops, and harvest the grain.

You can do this on a small scale in your garden, or in a large tub or window-box.

What You Do

1. If you have a patch in the garden, dig it over in either the autumn or in spring.

Remove any big stones, and break up the soil to make a fine **tilth** with your spade.

2. You need to plant your seeds in the spring.

Wheat or barley can be grown but try oats first. You should be able to get your oats from a farm, a riding school or a pet shop. Treated porridge oats will not grow.

3. Plant the seed in neat rows, about 2 cm. deep and 2 cm apart.

Keep the bed weed-free, being careful to work between the rows.

4. Wait and watch the plants until the heads are golden. This will take several months, so this is a long term experiment.

5. Cut the heads carefully, and 'winnow' the grain. You can do this with your hands, rubbing the grain and blowing away the chaff.

A farmer has to have machinery to do this. Early man used one stone on top of another to separate and grind the grain.

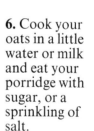

6. Cook your oats in a little water or milk and eat your porridge with sugar, or a sprinkling of salt.

27

PLANNING A NATURE TRAIL IN YOUR GARDEN

You do not need a large garden or a big space to be able to make a nature trail and turn your garden into a small nature reserve. If you have only a very small area, you can choose the smaller objects of interest, say a hanging bird feeder instead of a big bird table, and some pots of plants if your garden beds are small.

What You Do

1. First of all, make a list of all the interesting things already in your garden. There may be lots of things you haven't noticed.

2. Do you have a bird table? How many different kinds of birds visit it? Can you recognise any of them?

3. Have you got a little Christmas tree which you planted? Have you measured it each Christmas to see how much it grows each year?

4. Is there a little patch of nettles in your garden where butterflies can lay their eggs?

5. Does a robin or a blackbird use one of your gateposts or pillars as a song post?

6. Are there plants in your garden like Michaelmas Daisies or a Buddleia bush, that attract butterflies?

7. Have you found an **old** bird's nest? Look for nests in winter when trees and hedges are bare.

DO NOT DISTURB

8. Is there a patch of moss or lichen growing on a wall or on a tree trunk?

9. Have you any plants like honeysuckle or foxgloves growing which attract bees?

There are other interesting things you can add to your garden to make your nature trail busy and exciting.

Here are a few suggestions:—

1. A bird bath, perhaps a shallow pan or dustbin lid. Birds need water.

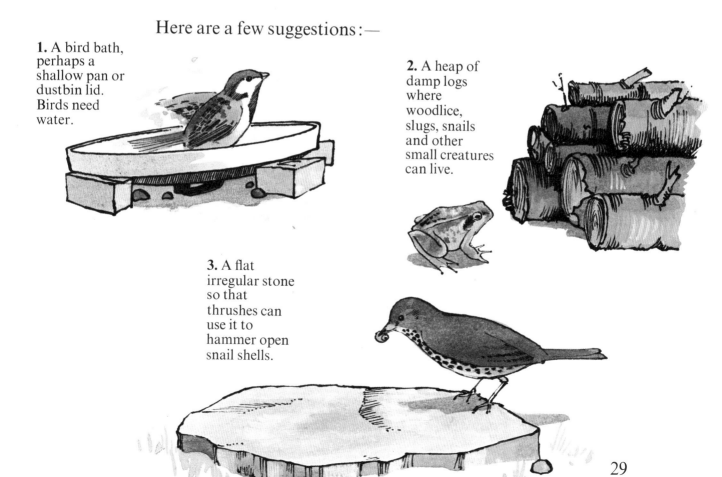

2. A heap of damp logs where woodlice, slugs, snails and other small creatures can live.

3. A flat irregular stone so that thrushes can use it to hammer open snail shells.

4. A collection of any odd objects found in your garden, for example, unusual stones, feathers, eggshells, any animal bones or pieces of broken pottery.

5. Can you persuade your parents to leave a small rough patch at the corner of the lawn?

Spiders, woodlice, beetles, centipedes are just a few of the animals that will live there.

Birds will be attracted by the insects, and bees and moths by the flowers.

Flowers like daisies, dandelions, buttercups and clover will grow there.

6. Put a bucket in a corner. Your bucket will soon fill up with rain-water and many tiny water animals will live there.

You may be lucky and be able to get hold of an old barrel to use as a water butt.

7. You could make a rain gauge and measure the rainfall.

All you need is a jam jar and a ruler. Hold the ruler against the jam jar every day and measure how much water there is in it.

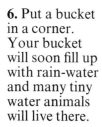

Distribute these extra items round your garden and plan the walk you want people to take, and which things you want people to look at. Then make numbered labels, with descriptions for each item, and place them, in order, on your route.

You can vary the trail from time to time. In winter there may be animal tracks; in spring, caterpillars on shrubs or trees or cobwebs to look at; or fungi in the autumn.

1. Collection of objects
2. Damp logs
3. Tree with moss or lichen
4. Bird's nest
5. Plants for bees
6. Song-post
7. Buddeia and Daisies
8. Nettles
9. Bucket for rain water
10. Flat stone

11. Rain gauge
12. Rough patch
13. Christmas trees
14. Bird table
15. Bird bath
16. Hedge

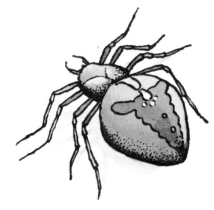

INDEX